IMAGES OF WALES

SKETTY

IMAGES OF WALES

SKETTY

DAVID GWYNN

TEMPUS

Frontispiece: General Baden Powell and the Hon. Odo and Mrs
Vivian at Glanrafon, November 1907.

First published 2004

Tempus Publishing Limited
The Mill, Brimscombe Port,
Stroud, Gloucestershire, GL5 2QG
www.tempus-publishing.com

British Library Cataloguing in Publication Data.
A catalogue record for this book is available from the British Library.

ISBN 0 7524 3380 6

Typesetting and origination by Tempus Publishing Limited.
Printed in Great Britain.

Contents

Acknowledgements

I would very much like to thank the following people, without whose help it would not have been possible to compile this book: Peter Muxworthy; Alan Pugh; Michael Williams; Berni Moore at the Bible College of Wales; Julia Ingham at Swansea College and Maxine Room, Principle of Swansea College; Revd Daniel Williams; Jan Platt at Olchfa School; Paul Bancroft; David Nicholas and Robin Blakely.

I would also like to pay tribute to the late Barbara John who was a Sketty girl through and through and whose fine collection of postcards, photographs and ephemera I was fortunate enough to inherit.

Lastly, but by no means last, I must thank my wife Alicia for her support and encouragement, and my children Caitlin, Rebecca and Steffan who have all helped enormously.

Introduction

Sketty is today a western suburb of Swansea, straddling the road from Swansea to Gower. At Sketty Cross this road crosses the road from Fforestfach to Blackpill, and, as is often the case, a village grew up at this important junction.

The origins of the name of the village have long been the cause of debate. Sketty may be of Scandinavian origin, or it may be derived from the Irish *St Cetti*, with a possible derivation from *Ynis Cetti*, 'the wood of Cetti'. A further possibility is a contraction of the Welsh *Is-Coed-ty*, meaning 'house in the lower wood'.

Norman Thomas tells us that in 1332 mention is made, in the foundation deed of St David's Hospital, of a watermill at Est Ketti. Sketty, therefore, seems to have a long history. Norman Thomas also reports references to the Singleton estate as early as 1319.

It seems that Sketty remained a small village until the nineteenth century, when a number of Swansea's most prominent citizens began establishing country seats in the area. John Henry Vivian, the copper magnate, built Singleton Abbey. Other large houses included Derwen Fawr, Glynderwen and Sketty Isaf, all later to be included in the Bible College of Wales. Sketty Park House was built in 1805 by Sir John Morris of Clasemont, Morriston. Vivian family members also lived at Parc Wern and Glanyrafon.

Sketty Hall was occupied by several families over the years, including those of Charles Baring Jr, Lewis Weston Dillwyn, Frank Ash Yeo and Richard Glynn Vivian, whose brother W. Graham Vivian lived at Clyne Castle.

Other houses included Hafod, Bloomfield, Pant Gwyn, Brynheulog, Pant-y-syfi and Penybryn. All these houses meant that Sketty's population included a large number of domestic servants. There were also a number of self-employed people involved in milk rounds, horse dealing, shopkeeping etc. There were more than twenty gardeners, market gardeners and nurserymen in the area. Farming remained an important activity in the area well into the twentieth century, as was the calling of publican.

On each corner of Sketty Cross could be found a public house. In 1856 the landlord of the Cross Inn was G. Fowler; the New Inn was run by W. Williams; at the Bush, E. Jones was in charge and mein host of the Vivian Arms was S.P. James. Today the Bush and the Vivian Arms continue to serve the people of Sketty.

Despite being well served by public houses, Sketty folk always seemed to be largely a God-fearing people. Non-conformity was established in the area in the seventeenth century, and the Temperance Movement was strong in the nineteenth and early twentieth century. Sketty boasts an impressive list of places of worship: Bethel Welsh and Bethel English Congregational churches; Sketty Methodist church; Seventh Day Adventist church; English Baptist church; St Benedict's Roman Catholic church and St Paul's church, Sketty; All Souls church, Tycoch and Holy Trinity church, Sketty Park.

Throughout the nineteenth century, Sketty was considered to be a rural area surrounding a pretty village where most of Swansea's prominent citizens had residences. The industrialisation that made Swansea one of the British Empire's great commercial centres bypassed Sketty, touching only the Clyne Valley where a few coalmines were established.

This rural isolation gradually was eroded as Swansea's westward expansion first touched and then engulfed the village. The twentieth century saw the building of large housing estates at Sketty Park, Cwmgwyn, Tycoch and Derwen Fawr. The last years of that century and the early years of the twenty-first century have seen a lot of infill, where small plots of land have been bought up by developers keen to build eight or ten houses in exclusive developments. Mandinam Park and Park Beck are two examples of this trend. As a result, Sketty today has a high density of housing and a large commuter population. Hence the nature of the area has changed, and Sketty can no longer be considered a rural area.

In this book, I aim to show aspects of Sketty over the years through pictures, post-cards, photographs and other interesting items. I have taken the liberty of starting this book at Clyne and Blackpill, although they lie outside the area that today we would consider to be Sketty. This I have done so that there is some continuity from my previous book in this series *Images of Wales: Mumbles*, which encompassed West Cross but no further.

I have divided this book into five chapters, the first of which is devoted to Clyne, Blackpill and Lower Sketty. The other chapters deal with Sketty Park, Sketty Woodlands, Singleton Park and Tycoch. The suburbanisation of Sketty through the twentieth century has meant that its boundaries are much less clear today than in the past. For my purposes Olchfa is the western boundary, Glanmor School and St Benedict's church mark the eastern edges, while the sea in the south and Llwynmawr to the north of Tycoch complete the area. I can only apologise to those who feel that these boundaries are either too restrictive or too generous.

I trust that you will enjoy this look at Sketty over the past one hundred years or so. I will conclude by reiterating my appeal from earlier books – if you find any old photographs of this area, or indeed any other, please do not allow them to be destroyed. Photographs are valuable social documents and must be preserved if our children and grandchildren are to have any idea of what life was like in the past.

David Gwynn

June 2004

one

Clyne,
Blackpill
and
Lower Sketty

Woodland Castle 1824. The original house at Clyne, called just Woodlands, was built in 1791 by Richard Phillips. Its purchase by General George Warde in 1800 began a twenty-year reconstruction of the house to create the neo-Gothic Woodlands Castle shown above.

In 1860 William Graham Vivian bought the Woodlands estate. He was a scion of the Vivian family of industrialists who in no small part contributed to making Swansea the leading metallurgical centre in the world.

Graham Vivian extended the castle considerably in the 1860s, adding the Great Hall, the north-east wing and a conservatory. In 1870, he changed the name of the castle to Clyne Castle.

As he grew older, Graham Vivian concluded that he needed a chapel on his estate, and duly began construction of Clyne chapel, adjacent to Mayals Road. The chapel was completed in 1907 and opened for worship in 1908.

CLYNE CHAPEL.
BLACKPILL.

Inside his chapel, Graham Vivian placed items that he had collected from southern Europe. The altar was made from Sicilian marble; the pulpit came from Rome and dated from the Renaissance, while six Siennese candlesticks, a chalice from Portugal and a bell from Spain furnished the altar.

In 1952, Clyne Castle and its grounds were purchased by Swansea Borough Council following the death of Admiral Walker-Heneage-Vivian, who had inherited the property in 1921. The castle itself was sold in 1955 to the University College of Swansea and the gardens retained as a public park. The Lodge, shown here in 1905, still stands at the entrance to the gardens.

Clyne Castle received many illustrious visitors during its history, especially during Graham Vivian and Admiral Walker-Heneage-Vivian's periods of ownership. Here the Admiral greets prime minister Stanley Baldwin at High Street station, before travelling down to Clyne.

Above: Winston Churchill was another guest of the Admiral at Clyne. Conservative politicians and members of the Royal family were frequent guests. The gentleman on the far right in this photograph is known to be Lord Kylsant.

Left: As a leading member of Swansea society, the Admiral held a number of high offices, including High Sheriff of Glamorgan in 1926, and deputy-lieutenant of the county. In this photograph he is seen in conversation with Edward Latham Bevan, first Bishop of Swansea and Brecon.

Clearly on his way to an important function, the Admiral poses in uniform next to his motor car. He is accompanied by his liveried chauffeur and footman, and is attended by his ever-faithful dog.

The early years of the twentieth century have been dubbed the golden age of picture postcards. The popularity of the postcard meant that many cards were published, with some views appearing with great frequency. One such was the Old Roman Bridge at Blackpill, shown here on a card published around 1910.

This early twentieth-century postcard of Mumbles Road, Blackpill shows the terrace of houses on the right-hand side, which still exist today, with the post office and stores still open. Just past the trees beyond is the Wodman Inn, but opposite, the houses have given way to a petrol station, and the widened road is very much busier.

This view, also from the early twentieth century, shows more clearly the terrace only partly seen in the previous picture.

TELE PHONE MUMBLES 209.   CUSTOMERS' CARS ARE STORED & DRIVEN AT OWNERS' RISK ONLY.   ESTABLISHED 1876.

BLACKPILL GARAGE, BLACKPILL, SWANSEA.

Mr. Howells. Bible College.   June 30 1925

DR. TO

TYRES, ACCESSORIES.
PETROL, OILS, ETC.,
STOCKED.

D. Lloyd & Co.

WIRELESS
ACCUMULATORS AND
STARTER BATTERIES
SUPPLIED AND
RECHARGED.
E. & O. E.

ALL CAR REPAIRS
A SPECIALITY.

COACH & MOTOR BODY BUILDERS
MOTOR AND CYCLE ENGINEERS.

Nov 1	Car Glyn Derwin to High Pt. Station.		5	6
18	1 qt Linseed Oil 2/1½, 1½ galls Aviation Petrol 3/6		5	1½
23	2½ lbs Brunswick Green @ 9d	1	10½	
	1 gall Linseed Oil		8	6
24	7 lbs of Carbide @ 5d		2	11
Dec 7	2. 3/8 set screws.			6
12	1 gall of Paraffin @ 1/3		1	3
13	Car Glyn Derwin to High Pt. Station.		5	0
20	Car Glyn Derwin to High Pt. Station		5	0
1925 22	7 lbs of Carbide 2/11, 1 Duplex Lamp Glass 1/6		4	5
Jan 5	1 gall Paraffin @ 1/3		1	3
7	Repairing top of Register Grate		5	0
12	7 lbs of Carbide		2	11
27	Sawing timber.		1	0
	1 gall Linseed Oil 8/6, 1 gall Paraffin 1/3		9	9
		£2	19	6

Date June 30th   No. 231
FOLIO No 51. New Series
Name Mr R. Howells. Bible College
Amount £ 2 — 19 — 6
D. LLOYD & Co.
BLACKPILL GARAGE, BLACKPILL
Per

Until recently, most businesses, both large and small, used beautifully printed invoices – the bill head often painstakingly engraved, as in this example issued by Ivor L. Davies, plumber, of Blackpill.

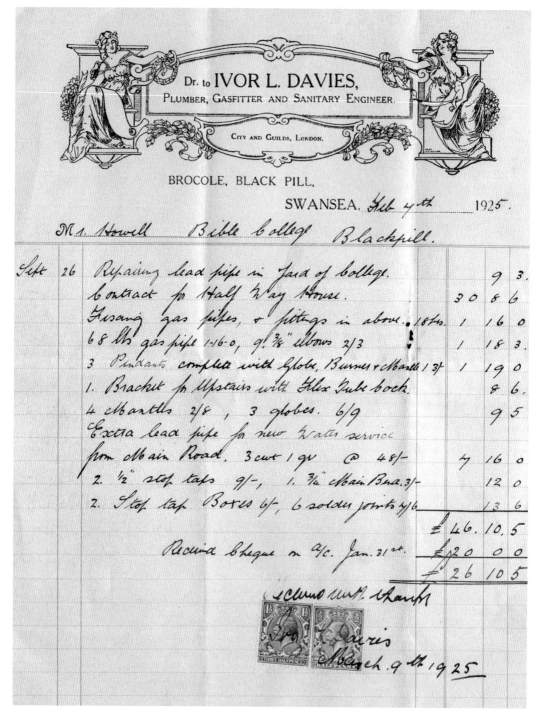

Dr. to IVOR L. DAVIES,
PLUMBER, GASFITTER AND SANITARY ENGINEER.

CITY AND GUILDS, LONDON.

BROCOLE, BLACK PILL,

SWANSEA, Feb 4th 1925.

Mr. Howell Bible College Blackpill.

Sept	26	Repairing lead pipe in Jard of College.		9	3
		Contract for Half Way House.	30	8	6
		Fixing gas pipes, & fittings in above. 18hrs	1	16	0
		68 lb gas pipe 1-16-0, 9 3/8" elbows 2/3	1	18	3
		3 Pendants complete with Globe, Burner & Mantle 13/	1	19	0
		1. Bracket for Upstairs with Flex Tube bock.		8	6
		4 Mantles 2/8 , 3 globes. 6/9		9	5
		Extra lead pipe for new water service			
		from Main Road. 3 cwt 1 qr @ 48/-	7	16	0
		2. 1/2" stop taps 9/-, 1. 3/4 Main Bena 3/-		12	0
		2. Stop tap Boxes 6/-, 6 solder joints 7/6		13	6
			£46	10	5
		Received Cheque on a/c. Jan. 31st.	£20	0	0
			£26	10	5

Another Blackpill business with a wealth of detail in its bill head was D. Lloyd & Co. of Blackpill garage.

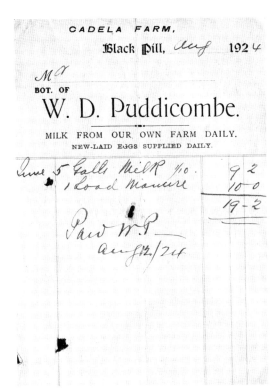

CADELA FARM,
Black Pill, *Aug* 1924

M
BOT. OF

W. D. Puddicombe.

MILK FROM OUR OWN FARM DAILY.
NEW-LAID EGGS SUPPLIED DAILY.

June	5 Galls Milk @ 1/10		9	2
	1 Load Manure		10	0
			19	2

Paid W.P
Aug 12/24

Mr W. Puddicombe provided milk and eggs
from Cadela Farm, Blackpill.

CAE-DA-LA DAIRY FARM

| Families Supplied with Milk and Eggs | | Milk for the Nursery and Invalids |

J. Evans

Dr. to **W. D. PUDDICOMBE**

Cowkeeper and Dairyman
BLACKPILL, SWANSEA

30th June 1925

Dr. Rees Howells

12½ Galls. milk @ 1/10   £1 2 5½

Another bill head from Mr Puddicombe
describes him as a cow-keeper and dairyman.

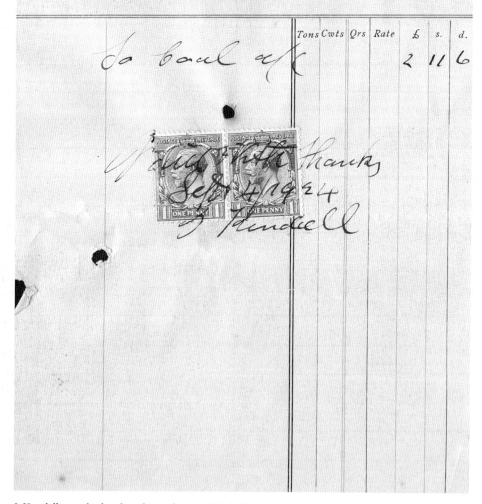

BLACKPILL, NEAR SWANSEA,

NAT. TEL.—56 MUMBLES ....*Sept* 4 1924

M *Rev. R. Howells*

Dr. to J. KENDALL,

Coal Merchant, General Haulier, &c.

Best Ffaldau Large and Nuts, and all other House Coals.

Anthracite—Large, Cobbles, Nuts and Beans.

MUMBLES AND SWANSEA.

	Tons	Cwts	Qrs	Rate	£	s.	d.
To coal a/c					2	11	6

Paid with thanks
Sept 4 1924
J. Kendall

J. Kendall was the local coal merchant at Blackpill.

20

Mill Lane, Blackpill, featured oft-photographed thatched cottages. The Mill, which gave the road its name, can be seen in the background.

The Mumbles Railway ran alongside the Mumbles Road from Rutland Street in Swansea to Mumbles Pier. From Victoria Station to Blackpill the LMS railway line ran alongside the Mumbles Railway, but then turned inland to go up the Clyne Valley to Killay, Dunvant and then on to mid-Wales. Beyond this bridge is Lower Sketty, better known today as Derwen Fawr.

Above: Postcard views of the Clyne Valley tend to show a peaceful rural idyll. However, in addition to a busy main railway line, Clyne Valley was home to coal mines, mineral workings and other small-scale industrial undertakings. Today the railway line is a cycle path and the woods have reclaimed and hidden the old workings.

Left: Derwen Fawr is today an affluent residential suburb of Swansea. Its name derives from Derwen Fawr House, which had been named after the enormous old oak tree that grew on the side of Bryn Road – the road that ran from Sketty Top Cross to Blackpill. When Sketty Park House had been built, part of Bryn Road had been rerouted. From around 1910 this road, too, took the name Derwen Fawr Road.

Glynderwen was the first property bought by the Revd Rees Howells in 1924, as the first step in the creation of the Bible College of Wales.

In 1929, Revd Howells added the Derwen Fawr estate, with the third property, Sketty Isaf, following in 1933. The purpose of the Bible College was to train missionaries to take the Christian message abroad.

This photograph shows the staff and pupils of the Bible College School in 1937, with the Revd Rees Howells and Mrs Howells at the front.

Opposite above: In 1933, Revd Howells began a school for the children of missionaries (who were not usually allowed to travel with their parents) at Sketty Isaf. So popular was the Bible College School that in 1934 it was removed to Glynderwen, which the Bible College had left in 1932 to move into Derwen Fawr House. The addition of new accommodation and class-rooms took place over the next four years.

Opposite below: In 1938 Prince Lidj Asrate Kassa, a nephew of the exiled Emperor Haile Se-lassie of Ethiopia, had enrolled as a pupil at the school. In 1939 the emperor came to Swansea to visit his nephew. In this photograph, students of the Bible College await his arrival

The emperor was given a civic reception by the Mayor of Swansea, Cllr David Richards, who appears on the steps of Derwen Fawr House in this photograph, with the mayoress, Revd and Mrs Howells and other civic dignitaries, students and staff.

The pupils of the Bible College School were not left out, as the emperor shook hands with each of them.

A few months later, in the summer of 1939, the emperor returned to spend two weeks camping with students and pupils on the Penllergaer estate, which Revd Howells had just purchased.

This photograph, showing a large group of people is, unfortunately, not dated. It was taken in front of Glynderwen which suggests a date in the 1920s, and possibly from the year in which the Bible College was founded. The mix of ages suggests that included are students, parents of students, possibly children of students, plus staff and other interested parties.

This photograph is dated 1932 and was taken outside Derwen Fawr House. As this was the year that the Bible College vacated Glynderwen and moved to Derwen Fawr House, maybe another gathering was arranged to celebrate the event.

Dating, it is thought, from 1938, this photograph was taken outside Glynderwen and shows the pupils and staff of the Bible College School, together with students and staff of the Bible College itself. Reverend Rees Howells and Mrs Howells are seated in the front row.

In January 1950, Revd Howells passed away and the directorship of the Bible College and Schools passed to his son, Revd Samuel Howells. In this early 1950s photograph he is seen with the staff of the college.

New building work was undertaken, along with the provision of additional facilities. Here, workmen dig the footings for the new gymnasium, which was in use by 1955, the year the Bible College School changed its name to Emmanuel Grammar School.

A new playing field was laid out at about the same time on a neighbouring marshy piece of ground acquired for the purpose. In 1977 it was refurbished as shown above.

Tennis courts were laid out at the same time as the field was refurbished.

These buildings replaced the old tennis lawn here shown in the 1940s.

The new fifth-form block was opened in 1974 and is the single-storey structure on the left in this picture.

In 1976 new laboratories were opened.

An annual event at Emmanuel was the bicycle race from the school to Oystermouth.

The javelin being thrown at a school sports day in the late 1950s.

The three-legged race, probably from the same sports day.

Leapfrog also featured, possibly as part of an obstacle race.

In the early 1950s a large tree fell in the school grounds, causing Derwen Fawr Road to be closed. The college truck is here seen loaded with part of the roots, ready for disposal.

At the eastern end of Derwen Fawr Road, where it joins Sketty Lane, is Sketty Green. This piece of open ground used to be known as Bryn Common, for the adjacent Bryn House, which was designed as a Dower House for the Morris family at Sketty Park.

Sketty Green was a popular gathering place, and here is a rare photograph indeed, dating from around 1900. It is August Bank Holiday and both children and adults have gathered for a chapel tea.

two

Sketty
Park

Sketty Park House was built in 1805 by John Morris of Clasement in Morriston. The development of the copper works in the Swansea Valley had contaminated the air around Clasement, so John Morris demolished it and built Sketty Park from the stones. Sketty Park House itself was demolished in 1975.

Opposite above: These gates stood at one of the entrances to Sketty Park House. It is believed that they originally graced Muswell House in Muswell Hill, London.

Opposite below: This 1951 view was taken from a house on the northern side of Sketty Park Drive, looking across the fields to Gabalfa Cottage in the woods of the Sketty Park estate.

Gabalfa Cottage photographed in September 1953.

In the summer of 1956 some improvements were made including a new outside lavatory and a kitchen extension. Note the tap fixed to a low post alongside the new facilities. The cottage was demolished in 1965 to make way for housing developments.

The fields around Gabalfa Cottage were farmed right up to the time development work began. Here we can see the last haymaking in the field that is now the site of Admiral's Walk and Benbow Close.

The first preparations for the clearing of land to make way for housing development along Gabalfa Road, 1965.

Away go the first trees as the woodland is cleared.

Measuring up before getting the first foundations laid.

With the trees largely gone, work begins on laying out a roadway.

Earlier housing to the north of the Gabalfa Road development included high-rise flats.

Provision was made for a large new population on the Sketty Park development, including the Spinning Wheel public house.

Shops were also provided at the junction of Parkway and Sketty Park Drive. The post office shown here, which is called Parkway, has just had the threat of closure lifted, much to the relief of residents of Sketty Park.

Alongside the Spinning Wheel is Briar Dene, shown here in 1969, decorated in celebration of the investiture of the Prince of Wales.

The Parkway Hotel, seen in 1977. While it backed onto Sketty Park, the frontage was on Gower Road. The building is no longer a hotel, for today it is the Parkway Dental Day-care Centre.

The view from Sketty Park Drive towards Dillwyn Road.

Rhyd-y-Defaid Drive in the snow, January 1982.

John Armine Morris, the grandson of the John Morris who built Sketty Park House, disliked the place and so built a smaller house on the northern edge of his park and called it Hafod. The house did not survive very long, as it was pulled down in the last years of the nineteenth century. The site is now occupied by Parkland School.

Jasmine Close in the snow, April 1966.

In the north-western corner of the old park now stands Olchfa School, a large comprehensive school with an outstanding reputation.

This photograph shows the prefects of Olchfa School in 1976 with the headmaster, Mr Curtis Grove, in the centre, seated. Mr Grove was a well-respected educationalist, both locally and beyond.

three

Sketty
Woodlands

Cockle women from Penclawdd make their way through Sketty village as they head for Swansea Market, *c.* 1860.

Some forty-five years later and this photograph from the same viewpoint shows Sketty as still essentially a rural village.

The Cross at Sketty was – and indeed remains – an important junction. Most of the traffic from Gower into Swansea passes through Sketty, and at one time four inns existed at these crossroads. The Cross Inn and the New Inn have long since disappeared, but the Vivian Arms and the Bush Inn remain. This photograph dates from around 1905 and shows the Bush Inn as a two-storey building very much like the cottages alongside.

By 1912 the old Bush Inn had gone and a new three-storey mock-Tudor structure had taken its place.

In the 1920s and 1930s the Sketty Cross end of Dillwyn Road was widened, with redevelopment taking place on both sides of the road. Squeezed between the Bush Inn and Lloyds Bank can be seen Rice's grocery shop.

T.J. Rice established his shop in 1870. Here Mr Rice and his wife pose for the camera around the turn of the twentieth century.

Standing at the door of the shop in this early photograph are the three Rice sisters – Audrey, Marjorie and Dulcie.

This photograph seems to date from around 1910, and it is believed that the man in the upstairs window is Harry Muxworthy. The Muxworthy's were a well-known family in Sketty, being particularly involved with the activities of Sketty Methodist church.

By the 1940s, the shop had been transformed with a new front. Interestingly, the blackboard in the doorway advertises New Gower Potatoes: 6lb for 1s 8d. This suggests that the photograph was taken in either late May or early June. The year the photograph was taken, however, is not known, although the notices headed 'Ryvita Crispbread' at the bottom of the right-hand window refer to wartime packaging, so probably it was taken either during the war or in the immediate post-war period.

The staff were photographed in the 1960s – and were from left to right: Reg Randall, the manager; Joan ?; Irene Hoare; Lillian Davies and Pam ?. The shop also employed a baker by the name of Bill. Rice's closed at the end of the 1960s. The neighbouring Lloyds Bank has also gone, having moved to new premises on the opposite side of Gower Road.

Rice's and the bank premises were redeveloped to create a Spar shop, seen here adjacent to the Bush.

Above: Dating from the 1950s, this view shows Gower Road looking east, in the direction of Swansea.

Left: An advertisement for the Odeon cinema which was placed in the local newspaper in 1958. Opened in November 1938 as the Maxime cinema, it became the Odeon in August 1944. In the 1960s it became a bingo hall.

At the end of the 1990s the bingo hall closed and the site was purchased by McCarthy & Stone. With additional building on the car park at the rear, it became flats for retired people.

This very early postcard shows the buildings on Gower Road, below the Eversley Road junction. At this time the Bush had not been redeveloped. The shop in the foreground is Sketty post office. A post office first opened in Sketty around 1849.

Left: On 8 July 1972, the Dillwyn Road building became a dedicated sorting office, and the post office was transferred to new premises on Gower Road. A further move, across the road, has brought the post office to its current premises.

Below: The sorting office in Dillwyn Road has now closed and the building is currently Maxim's fish and chip shop and Chinese takeaway.

Although evident in 1964, the wooden bus shelter outside the Court Library bookshop on Sketty Cross has long since vanished.

Heavy snow in January 1982 brought traffic to a standstill and led to queues for bread and other essentials outside the Spar shop in Sketty. Notice the cabbage crates stacked up outside Colin Jones' greengrocers shop on the left-hand side in the picture.

Dillwyn Road around 1910, looking towards Sketty Cross.

Dillwyn Road, again around 1910, looking away from Sketty Cross towards Sketty Park.

Above: The Sketty Park end of Dillwyn Road in more detail with Sketty Methodist church on the left, *c.* 1910.

Left: Sketty Methodist church in close-up. Built in 1876 and renovated in 1901, this building replaced 'the old chapel on the hill' on Gower Road.

St Paul's church, Sketty. This was built in 1850 by John Henry Vivian of Singleton Abbey and his eldest son Henry Hussey Vivian as a memorial to Henry Hussey's wife Jessie who died in 1848, subsequent to childbirth.

The porch of St Paul's church. In 1908 this porch was dismantled to allow for the building of a new north aisle, and then re-erected in its new, and current, position.

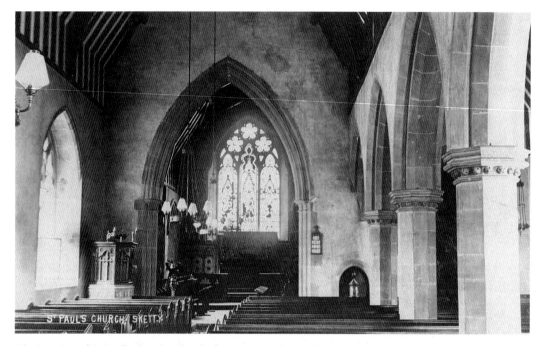

The interior of St Paul's church, taken before 1908, as the north aisle had not yet been built.

St Paul's church photographed in the snow, probably during the winter of 1906-07.

The lych gate of St Paul's church, *c.* 1900.

---THE---

Sketty Recipe Book

ISSUED IN CONNECTION WITH

The Sketty Vicarage Fund Bazaar

HELD AT

THE ALBERT HALL, SWANSEA.

12th and 13th OCTOBER, 1910.

... EDITED BY ...

The Honourable Mrs. VIVIAN & Miss LINDSAY.

In 1910 it was decided to build a new vicarage, and fund-raising efforts were undertaken. These included the publication of a recipe book, with recipes and handy hints provided by the ladies of Sketty.

Opposite: Reverend Cecil Lillingston, Vicar of Sketty 1903-08.

Reverend H.J. Stewart, Vicar of Sketty 1915-41. He became Archdeacon Stewart in 1941 and left the parish to go and serve in Brecon.

ORDER OF SERVICE

FOR THE

Re-Dedication of the Bells

IN

Saint Paul's Church
Sketty

ON

Saturday, September 23rd, 1950

AT

3.30 P.M.

The cover of the programme for the Order of Service held on 23 September 1950 to mark the rededication of the church bells.

The Parish Church of Sketty
Dedicated to Saint Paul
was Consecrated on
27th September, 1850
By the Lord Bishop of Saint David's

Wednesday, 27th September, 1950

ORDER OF SERVICE

PROCESSIONAL HYMN 393

PSALMS 96 AND 150

1ST LESSON : 1 KINGS 8, 22-40

MAGNIFICAT

2ND LESSON : JOHN 2, 13-22

NUNC DiMITTIS

ANTHEM—" THE HEAVENS ARE TELLING " (*Haydn*)

ADDRESS BY THE

Right Reverend the Lord Bishop of Worcester

HYMN 306
(COLLECTION)

" HALLELUJAH CHORUS " (*Handel*)

BLESSING

LAST VERSE OF HYMN 3

The cover of the Order of Service for the special service held to mark the centenary of the consecration of the church.

The old Church School which had been built in 1853. The building ceased to be a school in 1930 and was subsequently used as a hall and given the title of Church Institute. In 1937 a presentation was made to Revd Stewart to mark the twenty-first anniversary of his vicariate. He gave the money back to the church and it was used to extend the Church Institute, which now became the Stewart Hall.

By the late 1970s it was becoming clear that the Stewart Hall was less and less suited to the needs of the parish. Traffic levels on Gower Road had grown, and the hall itself was becoming too expensive to maintain. In 1988 the decision was made to sell, and this was done the following year. The whole site has been made into sheltered flats for the elderly.

Sketty Church School, *c.* 1886.

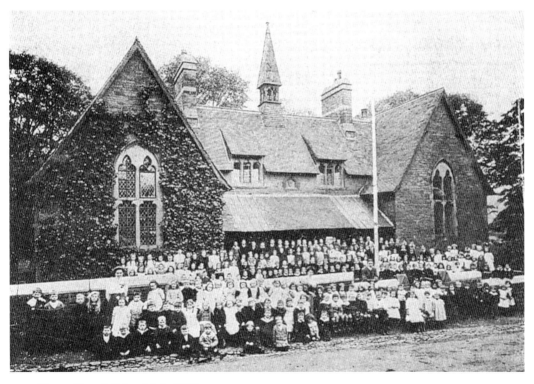

Sketty Church School, July 1909.

St Paul's church Mother's Union on a visit to Longleat in 1952.

Opposite above: The St Paul's church Dramatic Society have presented many plays over the years. The stalwarts of the society in the 1950s and 1960s are seen here performing *Leap in the Dark.* They are, at rear, from left to right: Bryan Roberts, Margot Ellis, Ennis Hughes, Ken Matthews, Jean Morgan, Edna Upcott, Barbara John, Ron Phillips. Front: Pauline Haines, Vic Davies and Ivy Matthews, who also produced the play.

Opposite below: In 1961 the production was *Bonaventure.*

Beside the Seaside brought the regulars together again, although the year of this production is not known...

```
                                                        "BESIDE  THE  SEASIDE"

                                                                  by
    The action of the play takes place in
    the Sitting-Room at "Seaview", a sea-                    Leslie Sands
    side boarding-house.  The time is the
    height of the summer season.
                                                     Cast in order of appearance


                                              Mrs. Austin  .. .. .. ..    Edna Upcott
            SYNOPSIS OF SCENES                Pat Marlow    .. .. .. ..   Margot Ellis
                                              Florrie       .. .. .. ..   Ivy Matthews
        ACT I:   Saturday.                    Tony Brett  .. .. .. ..    Glyn Bennett
        ACT II, Scene 1: Wednesday.           Ethel Pearson   .. .. ..   Barbara John
                Scene 2: Friday.              Wilf Pearson .. .. .. ..  Victor Davies
        ACT III: Saturday.                    Sally       .. .. .. ..    Ennis Hughes
                                              Mr. Pepper    .. .. .. ..  Bryan Roberts
                                              Mrs. Pepper  .. .. ..      Pauline Haines
             ----                             Policeman    .. .. .. ..    Alan Haines

    The telephone used in this play was
    loaned by kind permission of the                    Produced by Ivy Matthews
    Telephone Manager.
                                                                ------
             ----

        We would like to take this opportunity
    to thank our Patrons for their kind support.
    We do hope you will enjoy this family comedy    Stage Managers   .. .. ..   Alan Haines
    by Leslie Sands, and we trust that we may                                  Robert Morgan
    have the pleasure of your company at our                                   John Verrinder
    future productions.
                                              Electrician .. .. .. ..    H. Longhurst
                                              Property Mistress   .. ..      Vida Brown
             ----                             Wardrobe Mistress   .. ..    Barbara John
```

...we do have a copy of the programme, however.

One of Those Days: another critical success for the society.

SYNOPSIS OF SCENES

The play is set in the Sitting Room in the home of the Hallidays.

ACT I

A Saturday morning in August.

ACT II

Afternoon of the same day.

ACT III

Evening of the same day.

Stage Managers .. .. ..   Alan Haines
                             Robert Morgan

Lighting   .. ..   Alan Haines

Property Mistress .. ..   Mrs. V. Brown

Assistant .. ..   Anne Jones

The telephone used throughout this play
was kindly loaned by the Telephone Manager
Telephone House, Swansea.

"ONE OF THOSE DAYS"

by

KENT RICHARDS

Cast in order of their appearance:

JACKIE HALLIDAY ...	...	Ennis Hughes
GRANDMA (MRS. MOFFAT)	...	Barbara John
AMY HALLIDAY	... ...	Edna Upcott
MRS. BUNCE	... ...	Mary Taylor
GEORGE HALLIDAY ...	...	Victor Davies
MIRANDA HALLIDAY ...	...	Pauline Haines
HORACE BUNCE	... ...	Bryan Roberts
NIGEL EASTON	... ...	Robert Morgan
MRS. HARCOURT-PERCY	...	Jean Morgan

Produced by IVY MATTHEWS

We would welcome all members of the Parish
who feel that they would like to join in
any or all of the activities of our Society

Again, we are fortunate that the programme has survived.

Parc Wern had originally been a farm on the road between Sketty and Swansea. By 1817 it had become an imposing residence, and was bought by John Henry Vivian in 1840. It passed first to his son Hussey Vivian, and then to his daughter Dulcie, who allowed it to be used as a hospital in the First World War. It continued as a nurses' home until its name chnaged to called Parc Beck.

This 1930s view of Sketty Road, looking east, was taken from just outside Parc Beck, and shows the railings of the Parc Beck estate. From the Second World War, part of this land was devoted to allotments, with some fifty plots let and actively tended by keen allotment workers. In 1969 Norman Thomas was able to say that 'the Park Beck Society is rendering a valuable service as part of a national drive to increase home production and lessen unnecessary foreign consumption'. Sadly, the allotments have gone – after a hard-fought battle – and houses have been built on the site.

A plot of land at the eastern end of the allotments had been bought in 1926 by three prominent Swansea Catholic gentlemen, and in 1928 a church-cum-church hall was built to serve the Sketty area. In 1936 the Roman Catholic parish of Sketty was established with its own parish priest, Revd D.J. O'Keeffe. In 1953 a new presbytery was built alongside the church of St Benedicts. Seven years later, the building of a new church began on the remaining piece of land.

As the structure progressed passers-by could see that this was not going to be a traditional church building.

Designed by the Newport architects Bates and Price, the new church was courting controversy before it was finished. However, its modernity also brought praise.

With its unusual bell tower the new church dominated the neighbouring presbytery.

Above: By December 1961, the new building had been completed and now awaited opening. At this stage, however, it lacked one thing.

Right: That one thing was the controversial wrought-iron design occupying the front façade, representing the Pentecostal tongues of fire, the dove and the three-in-one of the Blessed Trinity. The completed church was blessed on 6 December 1961 by the Archbishop of Cardiff.

On 4 December 1975 St Benedict's was consecrated by the Archbishop of Cardiff, here seen third from the front in this procession after the service.

Above: The interior of St Benedict's church, 1961.

Left: The front cover of the Order of Service for the consecration.

Solemn Consecration

of

St. Benedict's Church,

Sketty, Swansea.

by

**HIS GRACE THE ARCHBISHOP OF CARDIFF,
THE MOST REVEREND JOHN A. MURPHY, D.D.**

on

THURSDAY, 4th DECEMBER, 1975 at 11 a.m.

Eversley Road, *c.* 1915.

Eversley Road, 2004. The
street remains an important
shopping street.

Bishop Gore School. Founded in 1682 by Bishop Hugh Gore, the original school thrived on Mount Pleasant Hill until 1952, when the present building opened on De la Beche Road.

The Lodge, De la Beche Road, photographed in 1970.

This rare photograph shows the Sketty lads who joined the King's Own Rifles in the First World War. It is not dated, but is likely to have been taken in 1915. The eleven are not named, but we do know that standing second from the right is Gerald Savage. The photograph was probably taken in the grounds of Sketty Hall Lodge.

Sketty Hall was built in the 1720s by Rawleigh Dawkins. It has been owned by a string of well-known local worthies, including Lewis Weston Dillwyn, owner of the Cambrian Pottery, scholar, naturalist and fellow of the Royal Society.

Right: From 1898 Sketty Hall was the home of Richard Glynn Vivian, who gave Swansea the Glynn Vivian Art Gallery.

Below: At one time, not long after purchasing Sketty Hall, Glynn Vivian purchased 187 cases of statuary and pedestals from a Genoan church in Italy and used them to lay out the Italian Garden.

The sundial in the garden of Sketty Hall, *c.* 1900.

The west front of Sketty Hall during the residency of Mr R. Glynn Vivian, who died in 1910.

The east front of sketty hall during the same period. In 1910 the house passed to the Hon. Mrs Violet Averil Margaret Douglas Campbell, a niece of Mr R. Glynn Vivian, and daughter of the first Lord Swansea.

The elaborate nature of the interior of the house can be seen in this late nineteenth century photograph of the hall. On the left above the stairs can be seen the back of the box that members of the family could use to watch plays in their private theatre.

Also in the hall, was a large model of a German house. In 1938 Sketty Hall was purchased by Swansea Corporation and was used for civil defence activities during the Second World War. A part of the grounds was used for the building of Bishop Gore School.

In 1947 the British Iron and Steel Research Association (BISRA) acquired Sketty Hall and the remaining land. It was officially opened on 3 July 1947.

This aerial view shows the extra accommodation provided for the research work carried out there.

Renovation work had to be carried out by BISRA to prepare Sketty Hall for its new role.

The workshop in the same year.

The staff of the new research laboratories on the opening day.

A member of staff uses the Taylor–Hobson Surface Meter. Much, although not all, of the early work carried out at Sketty Hall concerned the coatings applied to tinplate.

four

Singleton Park

The University College expanded dramatically, especially in the years after the Second World War. New buildings to the west of the abbey are seen here in the early 1960s.

Opposite above: John Henry Vivian bought the Singleton estate in 1816 and built a grand new Gothic-style house, which he named Singleton Abbey. This drawing appeared in the *Illustrated London News* in 1881.

Opposite below: In 1920 Swansea Corporation bought the Singleton estate, establishing a park covering most of the grounds. The abbey itself became the home of the University College of Swansea, a constituent college of the University of Wales.

By the end of the 1960s there had been a further phenomenal amount of growth.

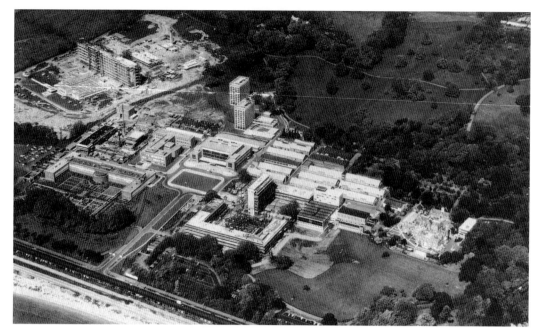

This postcard, which dates from around 1965 shows not only the University College but also, beyond it, the new Singleton Hospital. The outpatients department was completed in 1960. The second phase, incorporating the ward block, operating theatres etc. can be seen almost at completion, which was achieved in 1966.

Singleton Hospital has continued to expand, with a purpose-built maternity unit one of the most recent additions.

Singleton Park became a popular place with local people for strolling, dog-walking and picnicking, as can be seen here in this 1930s postcard.

From the first, the park was the venue for a wide variety of activities. This 1930s cricket match seems to have taken place on a sunny day, judging by the long shadows.

The Singleton Trails Races for trail bikes was on 7 August 1937. The mounted rider in this photo is a K. John, who eventually won the event with a chap called Edwards.

In 1907 the Royal National Eisteddfod of Wales was held at Singleton Park. The Gorsedd circle of stones erected for this event still stands and is seen here in around 1950.

The 1964 Eisteddfod was also held at Singleton Park, and enjoyed glorious weather.

Here, broadcaster, writer and journalist Alun Williams is seen outside the BBC pavilion.

Young Frances Button of Dunvant, dressed in traditional Welsh costume, poses outside the Urdd pavilion.

The Swansea Parks Department created an impressive floral display to mark the Eisteddfod.

In recent years, shows, concerts and other events have continued to be held in the park. This is the 1999 Party in the Park, sponsored by the local radio station The Wave.

Music for the older fans is augmented by activities for littler ones, such as this funfair.

J.H.Vivian's Swiss chalet still remains in the park, and is seen here in the snow in around 1965.

The walled garden of the old Singleton estate was adapted to form the Educational Gardens.

Greenhouses were erected to house collections of exotic plants, enabling the gardens to be known then as the Botanical Gardens. This 1964 view shows the greenhouses and the superb floral display.

The gatehouse of Singleton Abbey is at the bottom of Brynmill Lane where it meets the Mumbles Road. This photograph dates from the late 1930s.

five

Tycoch

Tycoch lies to the north of Sketty Woodlands, being centred around Tycoch Road and Tycoch Square in the early years of the twentieth century. This photograph shows the post office on Tycoch Road which was opened in 1910. In 1961 it was closed, to be replaced by Carnglas Road post office just off Tycoch Square.

A closer view of the long terrace of houses on Tycoch Road, probably dating from the 1930s.

Sketty Primary School dominates Tycoch Square.

Building work continues apace, in spring of 2004, to finish the new Sketty Primary School in time for the start of the academic year in September.

Mrs Bowen's class at Sketty Primary School, 1970. Mrs Bowen is the teacher on the left, with the head teacher, Mrs Price, on the right.

Sketty School football teams, probably photographed in the late 1930s or early 1940s.

Harlech Crescent in the snow January 1982. A very grey day.

New Bethel chapel, on Carnglas Road, around 1910.

Tavistock Road 1977.

Waiting for the Queen on Glanmor Road, during her 1977 Silver Jubilee visit to Swansea.

Left: Prince Philip waves to the crowd, Glanmor Road, 1977.

Below: Reverend Garfield James, with the servers and others, All Souls church, Tycoch, 1966.

Scottish dancers at the All Souls church fête, 1966.

The Scottish piper, All Souls church fête, 1966.

Reverend Robert Britton, Vicar of Tycoch from 1975 until his death in 1999.

Following page above: Swansea College of Further Education, which was officially opened on 12 March 1971. Work on the new college on Tycoch Road had begun in 1967, as the Old Guildhall building, which was then being used to house the college, was totally inadequate for such a role.

Following page below: Broadway, taken in the late 1920s, looking in a northerly direction, with no development on the horizon.

This photograph shows a scene from the late 1940s, by which time the housing development at Cwmgwyn had filled in the fields.

Glanmor Road, looking eastwards towards Uplands and Swansea, c. 1925. Glanmor School features prominently. The huts that made up much of the school were brought from Salisbury Plain in March 1921, with the school opening the following year.

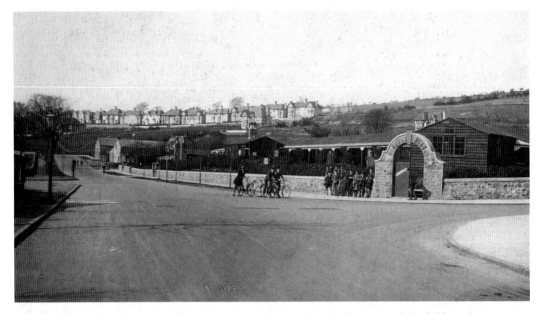

A closer view of Glanmor School, again from around 1925. The development of the fields in the background had just begun. Today Glanmor School has gone, and has been replaced by Lady Margaret Villas, Somerville Court, Newnham Crescent and Girton Villas. These names were the names of the houses at the school which, closed in 1973.

Some girls from the first, 1922 intake, relax in front of the camera in the fields behind the school. The boy in the background was probably not a grammar school pupil.

This photograph was taken at Swansea College just eighteen years ago, when the computer revolution was in its infancy.

A group of girls, who were part of the first intake in 1922, pose, I believe, with one of the teachers.

Other local titles published by Tempus

Gower Peninsula
DAVID GYWNN

This compilation of 200 archive images traces some of the changes that have taken place in the Gower Peninsula over the last century. The reader is taken on a tour of Gower as it once was, when local craftsmen had their place in every village, and families and communities worked together for the benefit of all. Each image is accompanied by detailed supporting text.
07524 2615 X

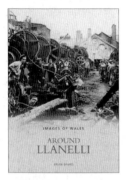

Swansea Town Football Club 1912-1964
PICHARD SHEPHERD

This collection of over 250 old photographs and assorted memorabilia illustrates the history of Swansea Town Football Club from its beginnings in 1912 until 1964, when The Swans came within forty-five minutes of reaching an FA Cup Final at Wembley. This book contains many action shots and behind-the-scenes pictures recording the formation of the club and the players that made the club great.
07524 1133 0

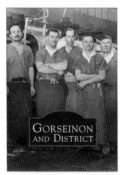

Around Llanelli
BRIAN DAVIES

Using over 200 images, Around Llanelli illustrates what life was like for the many varied workers – from tin miners to cockle pickers – who populated the area during the heyday of Welsh industrialism. In addition to the workaday world, the reader is taken on a journey around the streets, shops and social events and is introduced to some of the prominent characters from Llanelli and the surrounding valleys.
07524 3370 9

Gorseinon and District
KEITH E. MORGAN

This book charts the growth of Gorseinon and the surrounding district from a cluster of small agricultural hamlets into a thriving industrial community. It comprises over 200 archive images depicting all the different aspects of life in the area, from the pit winding gear and smoking chimneys of the local coal and steel industries to dance bands and day trips in charabancs.
07524 2859 4

If you are interested in purchasing other books published by Tempus, or in case you have difficulty finding any Tempus books in your local bookshop, you can also place orders directly through our website

www.tempus-publishing.com